SURVIVORS

SURVIVORS

A NEW VISION OF ENDANGERED WILDLIFE

PHOTOGRAPHS & TEXT
BY JAMES BALOG

HARRY N. ABRAMS, INC., PUBLISHERS, NEW YORK

PROJECT DIRECTOR: MARGARET L. KAPLAN
DESIGNER: RAYMOND P. HOOPER

Images selected from the present volume appeared in an international touring museum
exhibition. The project was produced under the auspices of the Black Star Publishing
Company, Inc., New York, and coordinated by Aaron Schindler, Photo Perspectives.
The photography was made possible in part by generous grants from the Professional
Photography Division of Eastman Kodak, Bronica, Comet Lights, and the Colorado
Council for the Arts and Humanities.

Library of Congress Cataloging-in-Publication Data

Balog, James.
Survivors : a new vision of endangered wildlife / text and
photographs by James Balog.
p. cm.
ISBN 0–8109–3908–8
1. Photography of animals. 2. Endangered species—Pictorial
works. 3. Balog, James. I. Title.
TR727.B25   1990
779′.32′092—dc20   90–31123
CIP

Published in 1990 by Harry N. Abrams, Incorporated, New York
A Times Mirror Company

Printed and bound in Italy

To the tide of evolution:
FOR MARY
FOR JAMES AND ALVINA
FOR KAREN AND SIMONE

The animal envoys of the Unseen Power no longer serve, as in primeval times, to teach and to guide mankind. Bears, lions, elephants, ibexes and gazelles are in cages in our zoos. Man is no longer the newcomer in a world of unexplored plains and forests, and our immediate neighbors are not wild beasts but other human beings, contending for goods and space on a planet that is whirling without end around the fireball of a star. Neither in body nor in mind do we inhabit the world of those hunting races of the Paleolithic millennia, to whose lives and life ways we nevertheless owe the very forms of our bodies and structures of our minds. Memories of their animal envoys still must sleep, somehow, within us; for they wake a little and stir when we venture into wilderness. They wake in terror to thunder. And again they wake, with a sense of recognition, when we enter any one of those great painted caves. Whatever the inward darkness may have been to which the shamans of those caves descended in their trances, the same must lie within ourselves, nightly visited in sleep.

Joseph Campbell, THE WAY OF THE ANIMAL POWERS

INTRODUCTION

ONE of the cherished illusions of our culture is that animals will always live contentedly in idyllic wilderness. Through television, magazines, books, and calendars, we feed ourselves an endless stream of imagery showing wildlife surrounded by glorious vistas, exquisite plant life, and technicolor sunsets. Such romantic imagery creates a sense that all is right with the world, that Eden is still out there, that the idyll will exist forever.

The reality of the present, not to mention the future, is radically different from this vision. In the temperate and tropical zones of the earth, humans have in fact destroyed much of the world's original habitat in a relentless search for farmland, living space, lumber, and minerals. As a result, the age of truly wild animals is nearly over. Unprecedented numbers of mammals, birds, reptiles, and amphibians are becoming extinct. Nearly 900 species and subspecies of animals are presently considered severely threatened, and hundreds more are under enough pressure to need considerable protection. These animals are the subjects of the photographs that follow.

Many of the species that survive this wave of extinction will be quasi-domesticated residents of wildlife preserves, where the ecology will largely be controlled by humans rather than by the traditional interaction among animals, plants, and earth. The remaining survivors will be captives, living in the artificial twilight zone of zoos. Their original wilderness will be reduced to enclosures landscaped by foam rocks; their "home range" will be surrounded by human dwellings and fast-food franchises; their mates will be chosen by computer selection; and their sex acts will take place in petri dishes.

Recognizing this, I have no desire to perpetuate the romantic mirages of traditional wildlife photography. Instead, I have created images of animals in exile from a lost Eden, adrift in the ether of a planet now made alien to them. It is a new kind of landscape, one largely devoid of the old, familiar topography. But it is the place they must now call home.

SOME of the photographic techniques I use to symbolize that new landscape were appropriated from contemporary advertising photography, whose contrived "look" is aimed at creating desire for superfluous consumer goods such as cosmetics, liquor, jewelry, and high-fashion clothing. In one sense, the use of those techniques is an ironic commentary on our society, which is so adept at turning the meaningless into the priceless.

In another sense, I use those techniques to separate the truly priceless from the meaningless. By changing the context in which animals are seen and by removing the visual distractions that usually surround them in nature and in nature-based imagery, I believe that we can freshly see their aesthetic qualities. We thus have a different basis from which to answer one of the crucial environmental questions of our time: Are these "objects" of exquisite formal beauty worth saving? I believe that they are.

The duality between the beauty of the animals and the horror of their present life was the initial impetus for making these images. But as the work progressed, another dimension developed as well. Over and over again, the best images embodied some intangible connection between the animals and me, as if a glass wall separating us had been broken. Sometimes, the wall would break because the animal ceased being a mute spectator and suddenly gave me a certain gaze. Usually, however, the most successful pictures resulted from a psychological response I had, a sense of recognizing myself in them. To use John Szarkowski's* metaphor, the picture became a mirror rather than a window. Even now, after working with so many animals, I do not consciously know how or why this linkage came about, but its effect on the photographs was profound. Because of it, I realized that this book was not simply a documentary about something outside myself, but was also about my life and my world.

Two remarkable writers, Joseph Campbell and Frederick Turner, helped me understand this symbolism. Though a full explanation of their ideas is well beyond the scope of this essay,** one of their central theses is that the philosophical heritage of western civilization, often called the Biblical tradition, has created a tremendous chasm between humans and nature. A brief passage from Campbell's *The Power of Myth* (p. 24) is worth quoting:

> In the Bible, eternity withdraws, and nature is corrupt, nature has fallen. In biblical thinking, we live in exile....When nature is thought of as evil, you don't put yourself in accord with it, you control it, or try to, and hence the tension, the anxiety, the cutting down of forests, the annihilation of native people.

IN this process of creating our exile, humanity cast animals into a philosophical abyss—and whether the animal was inside man or a wholly separate species, it was cast out just the same. In short, we became cut off from ourselves.

Photographs of animals in exile from their real lives thus refer to the exile of the human animal as well—rootless and confused, lost in a technological vacuum. There are many indications that we may finally be coming to grips with this

*Director, Department of Photography, The Museum of Modern Art, New York.
**For further information, see Campbell's *The Power of Myth* and Turner's *Beyond Geography.*

problem, and are realizing that human survival is possible only if we find a new way of thinking about our world. As we discover this new philosophy, we will automatically learn how to save many of the extraordinary and beautiful life-forms in this book from extinction. The tragedy is that our philosophical evolution will probably be too slow to save them all.

THERE is relatively little science in commentaries to the photographs. For one thing, that kind of information is available elsewhere. For another, scientific writing tends to put an animal in a glass box: one can see through the box and perceive the animal's outline, but one cannot feel its volume or its breath or its soul. Animals are reduced to relatively meaningless facts like gestation period and height.

The idiosyncratic commentaries speak of other things: of the encounter between animals and humans, of the individual animal's experience in this new alien world, of the artistic process, and of my own interaction with a particular animal. Perhaps through these image- and word-symbols, I can convey some part of the intensity of my time with these animal powers.

Because the tool of photography is a machine, photographers tend to become obsessed with controlling their medium. But in this project, willingness to abdicate some measure of control was essential. Working with external limitations, rather than against them, repeatedly produced surprising and constructive results.

MOST of the animals were photographed within their living enclosures at zoos and wildlife ranches, and the design of those spaces imposed severe limitations on our work. Animal behavior was of course even more of a factor. Though all the animals photographed for this volume were in captivity, the great majority had neither been handled nor trained, and their actions were unpredictable. It was thus critical to understand and accept the animal's wishes and emotions. Was he or she tired or energetic? Too hot or comfortable? Impatient, curious, or bored? Irritable or content? Skittish or placid? Were the background materials interesting or disturbing? How long was the animal's attention span? Usually it was twenty to thirty minutes but it ranged from no interest and cooperation at all to as long as an hour.

I usually started a session with an image in mind, but the combined difficulties of location and behavior made it nothing more than a point of departure. The issue of the animal's behavior was, in fact, of such importance that success or failure hung on a single question: What photograph was the animal willing to make *with* me?

ACKNOWLEDGMENTS

WHAT began as a lonely endeavor has ultimately received more assistance and support than I ever imagined it could: so many people, so many animals, so much cooperation from fate itself. To all, I am more grateful than I can possibly express.

Though they will never hear these words, I still must offer my thanks to all the fur- and feather- and scale-covered beings who worked with me, and to the people who so graciously provided opportunities to meet them. In addition to the institutions and individuals mentioned elsewhere in this book, I would like to thank the zoos in Colorado Springs, Sacramento, Fresno, Brownsville, Fort Worth, Gulfbreeze (Florida), and San Diego; and Moorpark College, The Cristiani Elephants, Kay and Duke Rosaire, Glenda and Bill Lassiter, Monkey Jungle, and the Denver Museum of Natural History.

Without the help of a few key people at certain critical times, this book would never have come into being. Howard Chapnick, of the Black Star photo agency, continually bolstered me with his confidence and enthusiasm. My parents, James and Alvina Balog, threw their support behind me during some very difficult times. When these images existed as little more than phantoms in my mind, Raymond DeMoulin and Marianne Samenko of Eastman Kodak's Professional Photography Division still had the faith to sponsor the initial sessions (in addition, they made the North American museum tour of the photographs possible). The Colorado Council for the Arts and Humanities also provided early funding. Hilary Araujo of GMI Photographic/ Bronica Division and Larry Farrell of ECOM Marketing loaned the tools to get my mental phantoms onto film. Margaret L. Kaplan and Paul Gottlieb of Harry N. Abrams, Inc., believed that a book of the images should be created. Finally, Wilbur Garrett, Thomas Kennedy, and Al Royce of the National Geographic Society were indispensable in bringing the series to a successful conclusion.

Through more blistering days and down more endless highways than I can count, Zachary Epps of Epigram Productions was much more than a technical assistant; he became a collaborator and friend. Equally, Aaron Schindler, project director for Black Star, was a companion through this journey.

To detail all the ways that so many others helped would become tedious, but my gratitude to them is no less profound: James Enyeart, Marianne Fulton, Robert Mayer, and Pat Musolf of George Eastman House, International Museum of Photography; Charles-Henri Favrod of the Musée de l'Elysée; Ron Egherman and Debra Heimerdinger of the Friends of Photography; Ren Hong Liang, Wang Zhao Yan, and Wang Zhu-de of the Chinese Photographers' Association, Shanghai Branch; John Echave, Kate Glassner, and Bill Graves of the National Geographic Society; Robert Adams, Renée Askins, Prince Bernhard of the Netherlands, Kevin Block, Cornell Capa, Rich Clarkson, Nicholas DeVore, Chuck Forsman, Frances Fralin, Larry George, Brian Lanker, Jane Livingston, Elizabeth Lui, Joe Marshall, Kent Meagher, Adriaan Monshouwer, Ken Paul, Robert Pledge, Bebe Price, Michael Rand, Sally Ranney, Alon Reininger, Meridel Rubenstein, Kevin Saehlenou, Marion Schut-Koelemij, Dieter Steiner, Kathleen Sullivan, and John Tennant.

My wife, Karen Breunig, and my daughter, Simone, were more patient, accommodating, and supportive than I ever knew was possible. I will never be able to thank them enough.

KEY TO PHOTOGRAPHS

Three agencies compile lists of endangered wildlife, each using different criteria. For the most seriously threatened animals, the opinions of the three agencies are virtually identical, but there is some discrepancy when it comes to the status of the less pressured species. Some of these animals may be on one list and not another. I have used all three lists to select the subjects for this volume. At the beginning of each commentary I have noted its status at the time of writing according to the three agencies.

The abbreviations used for the agencies and the definitions of terms are as follows:

USFWS—UNITED STATES FISH AND WILDLIFE SERVICE

Endangered: In danger of extinction in all or a significant part of its range

Threatened: Likely to become endangered in all or a significant part of its range in the foreseeable future

IUCN—INTERNATIONAL UNION FOR THE CONSERVATION OF NATURE

Endangered: In danger of extinction and whose survival is unlikely if the various causal factors continue operating

Vulnerable: Likely to become endangered in the near future

Rare: Small populations which are not at present Endangered or Vulnerable, but which are still at some risk

Indeterminate: Known to be Endangered, Vulnerable, or Rare, but lacking enough information to determine which of the categories is appropriate

Insufficiently known: Owing to a lack of information, animals suspected but not definitely known to belong to one of the above categories

CITES—CONVENTION ON INTERNATIONAL TRADE IN ENDANGERED SPECIES

CITES I: Threatened with extinction
CITES II: At serious risk and might become endangered if trade is not controlled or monitored

DRILL

"Chuka." Photographed
May 17, 1989. From the
private collection of
Carmen Hall at the
Ringling Brothers and
Barnum & Bailey Circus,
Rochester, New York.
Thirteen-year-old male.
USFWS Endangered,
IUCN Endangered,
CITES I

Drills are on the verge of extinction in the wild. Their native habitat in the tropical forests of Cameroon and Nigeria has been leveled for timber and to provide new land for farming. Because drills not only raid crops but have a sweet-flavored flesh which is locally much in demand, they are extensively hunted. Entire troops can be treed by hunters with dogs; it then is an easy matter to shoot twenty or more at once. Only one relatively small sanctuary, the Korup National Park in Cameroon, still contains a significant drill population.

Approximately sixty drills are in captivity worldwide, but the success of breeding programs has generally been poor. Chuka is the only drill in North America (and probably the entire world) docile enough to photograph in a studio. He was born in the Atlanta Zoo of parents who are believed to have been wild-caught.

18

Two of the five subspecies of this gazelle, which lives in the thornbush of the sub-Sahara region known as the Sahel, are already extinct. Nine to eleven thousand individuals of the other three subspecies are believed to survive in Chad, Mali, and the Sudan.

In the competition for forage and water in the Sahel, where drought has severely stressed humans and animals alike, the Dama is losing out to domestic livestock. In addition, large sport-hunting parties, sometimes composed of 100 local royalty and visiting dignitaries, have been known to slaughter dozens at a time.

This elegant animal was suspicious of our photographic equipment. He floated into position, stayed there for a few exposures, and was gone.

D A M A
G A Z E L L E

Photographed November 7, 1988, at Fossil Rim Wildlife Ranch, Glenrose, Texas. Full-grown adult male.
USFWS Endangered,
IUCN Endangered,
CITES I

This animal is one of the few "animal actors" I used for this volume. His days are spent doing things like car commercials and feature films. It is many generations since his ancestors were in the wild.

His parents were spotted in the familiar tan-and-black leopard pattern, but it so happened that a recessive gene produced a nearly all-black cat (known as "melanistic"). Up close, it is possible to discern the spots within the black.

Being close to a leopard, even though this one was ostensibly tame and did everything asked of him, is not something I wish to do often. Rarely in the course of this work did I get such a sense of malevolence and danger from an animal; those yellow eyes glaring from that dark feline face seemed to embody the hostility.

When this picture was made, I was relatively new to the subtleties of working around animals and made a big— potentially fatal—mistake. With the leopard on the set, I asked my assistant to run for a piece of equipment in our van. He took my request literally, running off in full sight of the cat. The leopard, as is normal for predators, saw him as an interesting moving target and was virtually into a leaping attack before the trainer could calm him down.

L E O P A R D

Photographed March 15, 1988, in the mountains near Malibu, California. Six-year-old male.
USFWS Endangered,
IUCN Threatened,
CITES I

JAGUAR

Not long ago, jaguars were common from the southwestern United States to Argentina. But their extraordinary fur became an object of intense desire in the developed countries. Legal hunting prior to the early 1970s caused their initial steep decline; illegal hunting since then has aggravated the problem. With agricultural development in vast areas of tropical forest dramatically compounding the cat's problems, jaguars are now extinct or nearly extinct in much of their former range.

This jaguar was not only one of the most beautiful animals I have ever seen, but also one of the most surreal. These images are an attempt to do justice to both characteristics.

"Poncho." Photographed
September 26, 1989, at
Cougar Hill Ranch,
Littlerock, California.
Five-year-old male.
USFWS Endangered,
IUCN Vulnerable,
CITES I

ASIAN ELEPHANT

In few cases did I work with a species more than once, but I photographed elephants many times in search of the intangible mystery and power they emanate.

A S I A N
E L E P H A N T

"Anusha." Photographed
October 18, 1989, at the
Singapore Zoo, Singapore.
Female, age unknown.
USFWS Endangered,
IUCN Endangered,
CITES I

Fewer than 39,000 Asian elephants are left in the wild. Expansion of farms has isolated the animals in relatively small islands of habitat, separated by oceans of human settlement. The animals left in each island thus become inbred and, given enough time, will eventually die out. A more urgent problem, however, is that the islands of habitat often lack enough suitable plant life to support the herds. The starving elephants then raid the banana, coffee, or jute fields that surround them—and are killed for being pests. Since bull elephants are more aggressive and do most of the raiding, they are killed far more often than cows; as a result, the gene pool is crashing. In sum, wild Asian elephants are trapped in a downward spiral which many experts believe will result in their extinction.

Periodically, a sense of just how big an elephant is came from a curious and small thing. Standing ten feet away, I could clearly hear the rush of running water, as if buckets were being emptied; waterfalls were flowing from one holding tank to the next in her massive internal digestive factory.

The moist trunk (you can see up inside it as far as the light shines) feeling up my leg leaves a barnyard odor that lingers for hours. Up close, sounds transmitted down the trunk have the same shimmery echo as does a pipe held to your ear.

AFRICAN ELEPHANT

"Jenny." Photographed
October 6, 1988, at the
Dallas Zoo, Dallas, Texas.
Thirteen-year-old female.
USFWS Endangered,
IUCN Vulnerable,
CITES I

HIMALAYAN BLACK BEAR

"Bruiser." Photographed November 14, 1988, at Dave Richtman's Bears Etc., Grand Prairie, Texas. Eleven-year-old male.
CITES I

Scientific names are not known for their poetry, but *Selenarctos thibetanus*, meaning "moon bear of Tibet," does have some literary magic. It refers to the crescent-shaped chest marking of this mountain inhabitant, who lives at altitudes up to 13,000 feet in south and east Asia. Humans there generally view it as an unwanted competitor, but at the same time the bear is considered a useful resource. It is hunted for fur and meat (bear paw soup is a great local delicacy); various pieces, particularly the gallbladder, are prized on the Oriental medicine market; and people kill mother Himalayans in what is ultimately a futile effort to turn their cubs into pets.

In the mass and tension of the muscle in Bruiser's paw, there is an electric sense of his power. But he is a gentle, drowsy animal and ambles quietly around the set in response to small offerings of food. When we asked him to stand on his hind legs, the unexpected occurred; instead of appearing intimidating, he seemed to become weightless.

GIANT INDIAN FRUIT BAT

"Count Batula."
Photographed March 2,
1989, at the Jacksonville
Zoo, Jacksonville, Florida.
Three-year-old male.

Nearly 200 species of flying fox are known, and most of them are seriously threatened by habitat destruction. Because scientists have not developed reliable census data on many bat populations—and this, says one bat expert, is a result of a bias toward "cuter" animals—some flying foxes have recently gone extinct without ever being listed as endangered. On the island territories of the United States, and in various parts of Australia and Southeast Asia, the range of some species has declined by more than 90 percent, but they still have not been put on the endangered list.

On many islands in the Pacific Ocean, flying foxes have been vastly overharvested to supply meat to Asian and African cities, where people eat the bats' breast meat and wings. In Australia, flying foxes are killed wholesale because they feed on human fruit crops.

This particular species of flying fox is not officially listed as endangered, but since it is nearly identical to its endangered kin, is under some pressure for survival, and was tractable enough for my purposes, I decided to make an image with him.

Having been bottle-fed from infancy, Count Batula nuzzles and cuddles up to his keeper like a puppy. He is friendly even with us, much given to licking our hands for residual flavors of food and sniffing our hair for the fragrance of shampoo.

ATLANTIC GREEN SEA TURTLE

"Jerry." Photographed October 16, 1988, at Sea Turtles, Inc., South Padre Island, Texas. Fifteen-month-old male. USFWS Threatened, IUCN Endangered, CITES I

Since the European conquest of the New World began in the sixteenth century, this turtle has been over-exploited for its meat, eggs, oil, and skin. Its population has been drastically reduced or completely eradicated in much of its former range.

Jerry lives in a large tank in the backyard of Ila Loetscher, an endearing eighty-four-year-old known nationwide as "The Turtle Lady." Though some viewers imagine that this turtle is uncomfortable, Ila felt that with the cushion under its shell it was relaxed and content.

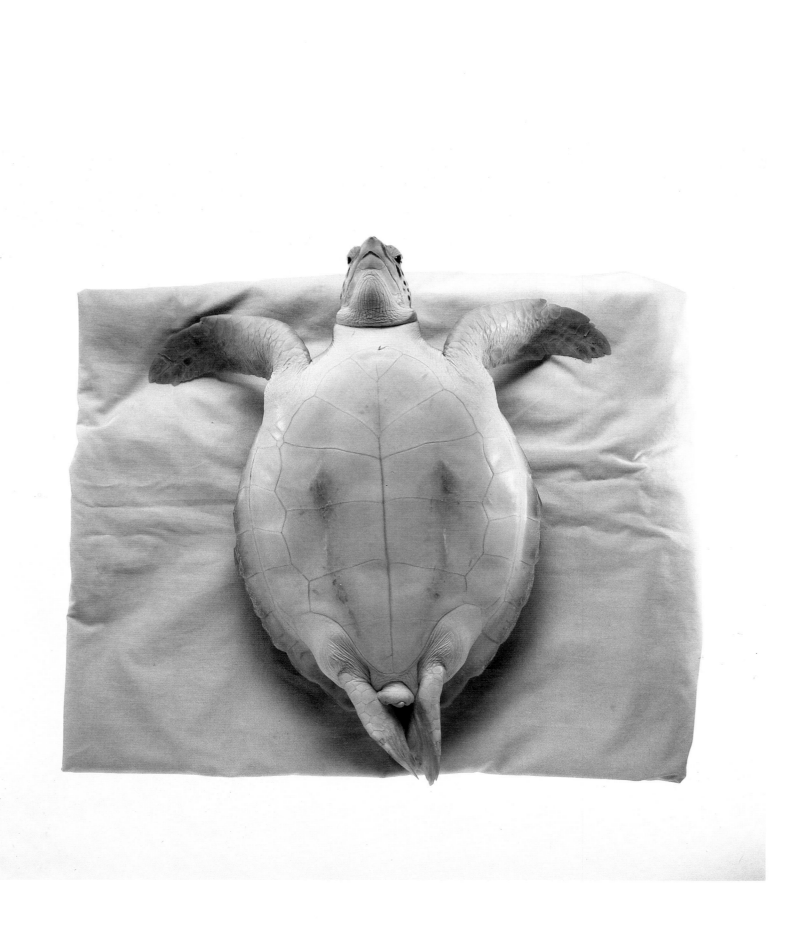

SCARLET MACAW

This species is still widespread through Latin America, but the pet trade and slash-and-burn agriculture have put considerable pressure on it.

Several sessions with various members of the parrot family produced no images which interested me—the photographs did not transcend simple prettiness or else they appeared cartoonish. But a found object in the landscape—the corrugated siding of a small ranch building—provided the basis of a quietly tense image.

Because humans are so self-centered, we tend to view war only as a human and cultural tragedy. In fact, war radically impacts wildlife as well. Hooded cranes spend the summer in central Siberia and nearly all of them winter in two small areas of Japan. At the start of World War II, 3,435 were counted on the winter range, but by 1945 there were only 250. The rest were apparently hunted by starving Japanese.

Largely because the birds' winter range was turned into a preserve, the crane population is now approaching pre-war levels. But the rice and wheat fields in which they feed are heavily sprayed with pesticides, and many birds have died as a result. If the winter range is destroyed, extinction is certain, for the psychological stress of captivity makes hooded cranes functionally sterile; during the entire twentieth century, less than five have been successfully bred in captivity.

HOODED CRANE

"Roto." Photographed
September 7, 1989, at the
Denver Zoo, Denver,
Colorado. Four-year-old
female.
USFWS Endangered,
IUCN Vulnerable

L A Y S A N
T E A L

Photographed November
11, 1988, at Sea World, San
Antonio, Texas. Six months
old, gender unknown.
IUCN Rare, CITES I

Laysan teal live on a solitary islet in the northwestern Hawaiian islands. In 1912, only seven individuals were left; European rabbits, introduced to the island, had literally eaten them out of house and home. The last rabbits were killed by 1923 and the teal recovered somewhat, but their populations are still small and fluctuate wildly. At one point, their fate teetered on the survival of a single remaining female.

When working with small animals, I found it nearly impossible to create the sense of landscape lost which underpins the images in this series. Here, I rendered that "landscape" with a huge Plexiglas salad bowl in the foreground. For me, it conjures up an alien world of the future.

Photographed October 25,
1989, at the Zoo Negara
Malaysia, Kuala Lumpur,
Malaysia. Adults of mixed
age and sex.
USFWS Endangered,
IUCN Endangered,
CITES I

MALAYAN TAPIR

No one knows how many tapirs remain in the forests of Southeast Asia, but it is certain that habitat destruction has made the animals rare or nonexistent in much of their former range. Tapirs taken from the jungle and transplanted to the open sunshine of zoos become sunburned—fur which normally is bright white becomes light gray.

"Jasmine." Photographed
March 12, 1988, at the
residence of Penny and Bill
Andrews, San Juan
Bautista, California. One-
year-old female.
USFWS Endangered,
IUCN Vulnerable,
CITES I

CLOUDED LEOPARD

During the warfare in Vietnam, Cambo-
dia, and Laos, bombing and defoliants
like Agent Orange killed many clouded
leopards. Simultaneously, the fur trade
was taking a major toll on cats living outside the war zone. With the fighting over
and new fur trading laws in effect, some
of the pressure is now off the cats. But
deforestation is still a major problem.

Most captive clouded leopards in
North America are descended from a single male, named Singa, who was wild-
caught in the 1960s.

Even the fastest animal on earth is defenseless against poachers armed with rapid-fire weapons. In recent years, as many as 5,000 cheetahs have been killed annually. Expansion of African farms has driven the cat from much of its former range, fragmenting the species into a few habitat islands. Some biologists believe that all the cheetahs left in those islands are inbred.

Rain drips from the eaves on a soggy spring day. We have made our set in a small classroom at the zoo, and tried a first round of photography with Hashim. Normally, says his keeper, the cat will go anywhere and do anything for a piece of Monterey Jack cheese. But as luck would have it, all he wants to do today is sleep.

Everyone leaves for a lunch break except Hashim and me. He flops onto the floor and rests his head against the cool cinderblock wall. We rest peacefully; the lights hum, and he purrs while I scratch his taut belly. He has been so uncooperative that I wonder if we will ever manage a decent picture. Another rainshower patters outside as Hashim closes his eyes and once more drifts off. The answer doesn't seem to matter; these moments are enough.

C H E E T A H

"Hashim." Photographed
May 22 and 23, 1989, at the
Columbus Zoo, Powell,
Ohio. Thirty-month-old
male.
USFWS Endangered,
IUCN Vulnerable,
CITES I

RING-TAILED LEMUR

Photographed May 20,
1989, at the Cleveland Zoo,
Cleveland, Ohio.
Mixed age and sex.
USFWS Endangered,
IUCN Unknown, CITES I

CHILEAN FLAMINGO

These birds, as well as several other flamingo species, are pressured by humans seeking feathers for decoration and meat and eggs for food. In addition, they are gradually being crowded out of the briny freshwater lakes they call home.

Aboriginal Australians believe that all life-forms, including those now extinct and those which are still to evolve, exist in a tangible space below the earth's surface. Perhaps the landscape of the flamingo netherworld looks something like this photograph.

Photographed January 28,
1989, at Sunken Gardens,
St. Petersburg, Florida.
CITES II

The scene was like a Florida tourism promotion: pelicans silhouetted by a golden sun dipping into the Gulf of Mexico, waves hissing against the sand, and palm fronds rustling in the breeze. But something was awry in Eden: a long tail of fishing line, complete with treble hooks, streamed from the rectal opening of a pelican. And so it goes with thousands of the birds, who swallow all manner of human detritus from bottle caps to chemical pollutants.

Brown pelicans are nevertheless one of the main endangered species success stories. In 1970, eggshell thinning from DDT had all but wiped out the species. But a few years after the chemical was banned, the birds began to reproduce successfully again and are now plentiful in much of their former North American range. In Latin America, however, commercial fishermen have so radically reduced the pelicans' food supply that they may not survive.

Pelicans appear to be from another era of the planet. In flight, they closely resemble the long-extinct pterodactyl. The mysterious and wonderful pouch below their bills is made of skin as thin and transparent as paper. The tiny feathers down their neck and upper back are so light to the touch that without looking I could not really be sure my fingers were touching them.

BROWN PELICAN

"Roman." Photographed
January 6, 1989, at
Suncoast Seabird
Sanctuary, Indian Shores,
Florida. Eight-month-old
female.
USFWS Endangered

WATTLED CRANE

"Boris." Photographed March 5, 1989, at White Oak Plantation, Yulee, Florida. Five-year-old male.
Considered de facto endangered by many specialists

This oryx's parents were caught somewhere in the Sahara, most likely in Chad. Samantha was born in Texas, in the Houston Zoo. She was born with a bad eye, and zookeepers took her from her mother when she was one day old in order to treat the defect. After a week of being cared for only by humans, both the parent and the herd rejected her. Naida Loskutoff, a scientist at Texas A & M, agreed to rear her. Loskutoff is now using Samantha in various innovative experiments in reproductive science.

Three years of drought, a war in Chad, and the expansion of the Sahara are pressuring the animals which remain in the wild.

SCIMITAR-HORNED ORYX

"Samantha." Photographed October 19, 1988, at Texas A & M University, College Station, Texas. Four-year-old adult female.
IUCN Endangered, CITES I

BONTEBOK

Photographed March 4,
1989, at White Oak
Plantation, Yulee, Florida.
Four-year-old female.
USFWS Endangered,
IUCN Vulnerable,
CITES II

These elegant savannah-dwellers once were widespread in the region now known as South Africa, but were indiscriminately slaughtered during the eighteenth and early nineteenth centuries. By 1837, only fifteen survived. These were gradually propagated into a herd of 800 ranch animals which live in South Africa's Bontebok National Park. Perhaps a fourth as many bontebok live in zoos and ranches elsewhere in the world.

Kangaroos, including the red, are slaughtered by the millions each year in their native Australian habitat. There, people see them as pests competing with sheep for grazing land. Though hundreds of thousands of red kangaroos currently live in Australia, they were put on the U.S. endangered list because American wildlife biologists believe such uncontrolled and excessive killing presents great potential for a catastrophic decline in their numbers.

Known professionally as "Killer Willard the Boxing Kangaroo," Joey performs in a mock boxing act at circuses. But he is really not much of a killer, being gentle and lethargic like all kangaroos and preferring to drowse in cool wallows he digs in the sand. He is induced to perform in the circus only by the rewards of food and kindness. His trainers say they never actually hit him because he, like other kangaroos, is so emotionally sensitive that after one blow "he would quit and never act again."

In spite of Joey's sluggishness, he projects an aura of coiled power. His tail, which is used for balance, is remarkably dense and heavy. There is something strangely unsettling about his sweat, which flows copiously on his chest and elbows: instead of being water-clear, it is red.

RED KANGAROO

"Joey." Photographed January 7, 1988, at the Fossett family home, Sarasota, Florida. Eight-year-old male.
USFWS Endangered

One day in 1986, Junior and eleven other eagles were relaxing peacefully in their cages on Mt. Apo, the Philippines' highest peak. Suddenly, artillery began roaring overhead as government troops bombarded Communist insurgents hiding in the rainforest. Believing that the army would not fire on the eagles, which many Filipinos consider a national treasure, the rebels fled into the vegetation around the eagle enclave. But the bombardment followed them, until the birds were in danger of being hit by shrapnel. At that point the center's director, Ron Krupa, raced downvalley to the artillery emplacement and pleaded with the commander to stop the barrage. Happily, he agreed, and the birds were spared.

Today, the island of Mindanao is still a hotbed of insurrection, with skirmishes and terrorism a daily occurrence. Shortly before our visit, thirty-five guerillas were killed in a firefight and two western missionaries were murdered within miles of our hotel. The eagles are somewhat safer, having been relocated to an area where the rainforest has been cleared and the secondary growth does not provide such good sanctuary for the rebels.

In fact, the modern Philippines provide little ideal haven for jungle fighters: less acreage remains of the original forests than there is in a moderate-size American national park, all of it fragmented into dozens of small areas that are dissolving in a tidal wave of loggers, slash-and-burn farmers, and plantation owners. The Philippine eagle has thus been in drastic decline and only 150 to 230 are left.

Junior was just a few months old when a logger chopped down his nest tree, captured him and, later, turned him over to the conservation center. The eagle now believes that his mate is a Filipino worker named Ben. Twice a day, Junior and Ben go through a mating ritual, which finishes with the eagle ejaculating on the man's surgically gloved hand. Though the semen is used in artificial insemination procedures, no eaglets have been produced to date.

PHILIPPINE EAGLE

"Junior." Photographed
October 29, 1989, at the
Philippine Eagle Research
and Nature Center, Dabao
City, Mindanao, the
Philippines.
Nine-year-old male.
USFWS Endangered,
IUCN Endangered,
CITES I

AGILE GIBBON

"J.J." Photographed
October 19, 1989, at the
Singapore Zoo, Singapore.
Six-year-old male.
USFWS Endangered,
CITES I

To a primate living high in a mahogany tree, the experience that we casually abstract into the word "deforestation" must be overwhelmingly terrifying: the invasion by aliens, the noise, the horror of home lost, the frenzy of disorientation. In the course of this warlike chaos, young animals are frequently separated from their parents and captured by the people doing the cutting. Such was the fate of J.J. somewhere in the forests of Indonesia. He was later confiscated by officials and turned over to the zoo.

Deforestation has put every gibbon species on the American endangered list.

BACTRIAN CAMEL

"Alfred." Photographed
January 24, 1989, at the
Lowry Park Zoo, Tampa,
Florida. Owned by Jo-Don
Farms, Frankville,
Wisconsin.
Five-year-old male.
USFWS Endangered,
IUCN Vulnerable

Though Bactrians will probably survive indefinitely in captivity, thus being reduced to cattle-like status, only 500 to 1,000 wild ones are left, and they are diminishing rapidly. Natives of the vast landscapes of the Gobi Desert in Mongolia and China, they are unable to compete with domestic livestock for water. In addition, humans kill them for their meat.

Bactrians' survival mechanisms are awesome, but they will become meaningless vestigial curiosities once the animals go extinct in the wild and perhaps no longer even live in deserts. An extra eyelid wipes sand off the eye; nostrils can be narrowed to tiny slits in a sandstorm; their body temperature increases 6 to 8 degrees Fahrenheit in hot weather so that they sweat less and conserve water. They can drink 25 to 30 gallons of water at a time.

This captive camel known as Alfred spends most of his life in subtropical humidity, plodding around a fenced oval track, giving $1.50 rides to suburban children.

TIGER

"Stosh." Photographed
September 22, 1989, at
Steve Martin's Working
Wildlife, Lockwood Valley,
California. One-year-old
male.
USFWS Endangered,
IUCN Endangered,
CITES I

PRZEWALSKI'S HORSE

Photographed
September 7, 1989,
at the Denver Zoo,
Denver, Colorado.
USFWS Endangered,
IUCN Extinct, CITES I

Some 12,000 years ago, someone now known only by the artwork left behind hiked up a hillside path and into a cave. He or she stroked charcoal across the cave's wall, making the first of many exquisite Przewalski's horse paintings in a place we know as Lascaux, France.

At the time, the horse was a common feature of daily life in Europe and Asia. But its flesh was tasty, it could not be saddle-broken, and it competed for grazing land with more tractable animals. By the end of the seventeenth century it had been exterminated in most of Europe, and by the end of the nineteenth century, only a few small bands survived in Mongolia. By 1968, they had been killed off by local herdsmen, and Przewalski's horse was extinct in the wild.

Today, approximately 680 of the horses survive in captivity, all of them descendants of only twelve horses trapped in Mongolia late in the nineteenth century. The likelihood of inbreeding is thus enormous and the horse may ultimately go completely extinct.

I understood only in hindsight that there were odd coincidences between my image-making experience and that of the primitive cave painter. Circumstance forced me to work in a windowless cinderblock room, a kind of latter-day cave. Then, the zookeepers warned that the horses would pull down any background material hung on the room's wall, so I decided to paint the wall itself (something I had never previously needed to do). As I worked in the dark, the lightbeam glancing across the animal forms was reminiscent of a pool of firelight flickering on a cave wall.

Tamarraw are a form of wild cattle living only on the Philippine island of Mindoro. Like so many other endangered species, they do not have a constituency in the developed world that finds them cute or cuddly or otherwise worthy of spending money. They are rapidly slipping toward extinction in the wild, and may survive only as domestics.

Blue smoke shrouds a decayed and decrepit landscape of rusted bars and animals slumped in the corners of their cages, half-dead with mental depression. If there were a nuclear war and any zoo survived, it would surely look like this one. Mary ignored us and aimlessly drifted around a pen backed by the monolithic facade of a bank building. Yet for just one second, the glass wall between us broke down.

T A M A R R A W

"Mary." Photographed October 27, 1989, at the Manila Zoo, Manila, the Philippines. Twenty-year-old female. USFWS Endangered, IUCN Endangered, CITES I

GREAT GRAY OWL

Photographed March 11,
1988, at the San Francisco
Zoo, San Francisco,
California. Three-year-old
female.
Endangered in California

MANDRILL

"Sumy." Photographed
May 17, 1989. From the
private collection of
Carmen Hall at the
Ringling Brothers and
Barnum & Bailey Circus,
Rochester, New York.
Seventeen-year-old male.
USFWS Endangered,
IUCN Vulnerable,
CITES I

Mandrills live in the thick tropical forests along the African coast from southwestern Cameroon to southwestern Congo. They are under intense pressure from the same forces besetting so many other inhabitants of the tropical forests; their homes are being destroyed by loggers, firewood cutters, and farmers, and their tasty meat is highly valued by local residents.

We had built our stage set in the musty basement of a huge events arena. Though the basement held an ark of circus animals, including 18 Asian elephants, 4 zebras, 14 lions, 11 baboons, 8 bears, 2 llamas, and 3 tigers, the place was quiet as a library. The background paper's simple white shape, forming a non-space within the room, was an island of tranquillity in the visual clutter.

Without warning, from around a corner tiled in institutional tan, a woman walked hand-in-hand with one of the strangest beings I have ever seen. Wildlife books and calendars like to reduce mandrill faces to bright, slick graphics, never doing justice to the visual power of these animals. For an instant, the brown eyes and primate bone structure made me think I had taken a quick glance in the mirror, but on the doubletake the intense colors and patterns suggested a drug-induced hallucination.

Hunched over, Sumy waddled onto the set. He glared at us and repeatedly bobbed his head in a threat gesture remarkably similar to that of young men who strut down urban streets posturing their dominion. Eventually, he climbed onto the stool and spontaneously posed himself.

Eggshell thinning caused by DDT ravaged the bald eagle population in the Lower 48 states; by the early 1960s, approximately 400 nesting pairs survived. In response to intense public concern, the chemical was banned in 1972 and eagle populations had climbed to almost 2,600 nesting pairs some eighteen years later. Though bald eagles will never again inhabit the range they once did, the species is now stable enough that it may soon be taken off the endangered list.

Ishi was once a wild eagle, but was wounded by gunfire from ignorant "sportsmen." Though she was rehabilitated and released into new habitat, she refused to forage for herself, and so she was recaptured.

We often think that zoos will be the salvation of wildlife, places to preserve the last survivors of a nearly extinct species until habitat conditions someday improve. However, captive animals never learn survival skills, forget what they once knew, or become too despondent to practice what they still know.

BALD EAGLE

"Ishi." Photographed
March 11, 1988, at the San
Francisco Zoo, San
Francisco, California.
Approximately fifteen-
year-old female.
USFWS Endangered,
CITES I

PINK PIGEON

Ring number 0023.
Photographed October 20,
1989, at Jurong Bird Park,
Singapore. Ten-year-old
female.
IUCN Endangered

On the day this photograph was made, less than a dozen wild-born pink pigeons still survived in their Mauritius Island habitat. The species has been ravaged by deforestation and the introduction of exotic plants and animals (mongooses and feral cats). In captivity, nine of ten pink pigeons are infertile, destroy their eggs, or do not know how to care for their young. Captive breeding efforts have achieved modest success only by allowing Barbary doves to act as surrogate parents.

Several dozen pink pigeons now live in self-sustaining captive populations on Mauritius, the Isle of Jersey, and Singapore. In 1984, a few of these birds were released into a botanic garden on Mauritius, but were almost immediately killed by boys with slingshots.

ADDAX

Photographed October 8,
1989, at Camp Cooley
Ranch, Franklin, Texas.
Male, age unknown.
IUCN Endangered,
CITES I

GREATER INDIAN HORNBILL

"New Delhi Dolly."
Photographed January 25,
1989, at Sunken Gardens,
St. Petersburg, Florida.
Fourteen-year-old female.
CITES II

"Noodlesnoot."
Photographed February
13, 1989, at Jungle Larry's
Zoological Park, Naples,
Florida.
Twelve-year-old male.
IUCN Vulnerable,
CITES II

GIANT ANTEATER

Anteaters are not overly fond of ants, but they do like ant eggs and termites, which they extract by flicking their two-foot-long tongues into the insect colonies.

Several major factors contribute to the animals' decline. South America's rainforests are being ravaged by slash-and-burn agricultural techniques and its wild savannah is being taken over by grazing cattle. The animals' thick hide is used for leather. And, in a bizarre twist to the extinction story, anteaters' tails are sought after for brooms and brushes.

DORCAS GAZELLE

Photographed (with
marabou stork) January
11, 1989, at Busch Gardens,
Tampa, Florida.
Mixed age and sex.
USFWS Endangered,
IUCN Vulnerable

OKAPI

"Chuma." Photographed
June 26, 1989, at the San
Diego Wild Animal Park,
Escondido, California.
Four-year-old male.
Considered de facto
endangered by many
specialists

To be put on the endangered lists, most species must have been studied well enough for biologists to estimate past and future populations. But some animals, like the okapi, are so elusive and live in such impenetrable landscapes that not enough data have been developed.

The okapi, which inhabits only the dark recesses of the Ituri Forest in Zaire and was not even known to science until 1901, is one such animal. Since it is definitely rare and is dependent on a single confined habitat, many African animal specialists consider the okapi endangered. The zoo community has developed a species survival plan for okapi, which is usually done only for endangered animals.

The species survival plan is primarily a computerized method of ensuring that the sixty-nine okapis in captivity worldwide do not become inbred. A pairing of this kind may not necessarily succeed, because mating between animals often depends on the kind of emotional chemistry governing relationships between humans.

GAUR

"Elroy." Photographed
October 12, 1988, at the
Gladys Porter Zoo,
Brownsville, Texas. Seven-
year-old male.
USFWS Endangered,
IUCN Vulnerable,
CITES I

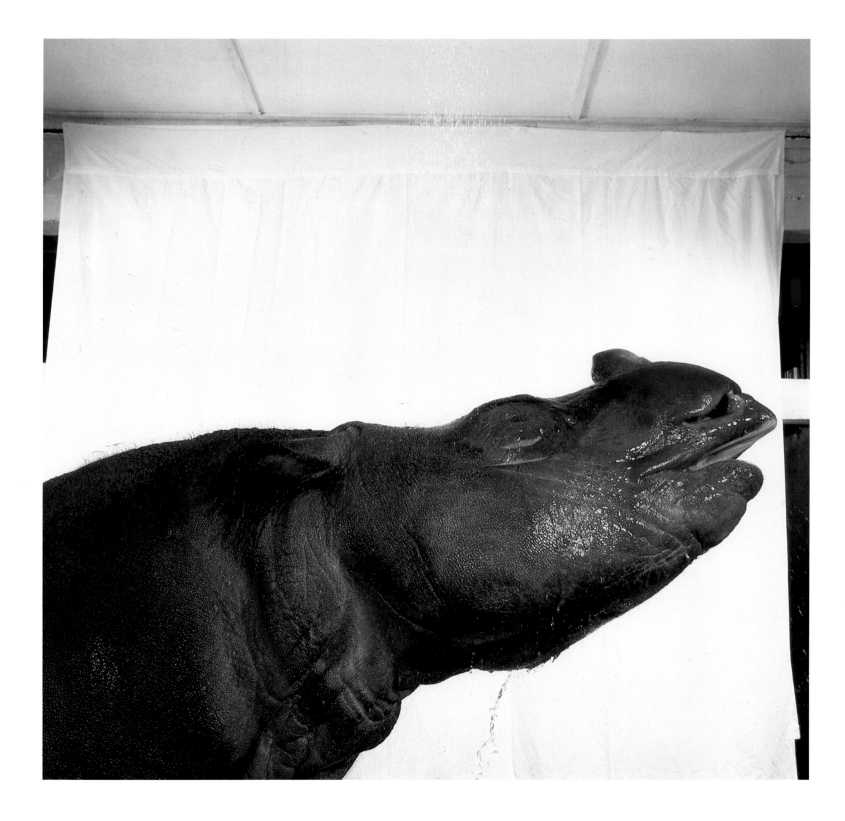

This is one of the most endangered large mammals in the world. Destruction of tropical forest and poaching have made the density and numbers of wild Sumatran rhinos so low that many biologists believe extinction is inevitable. In Malaysia, for example, only 100 animals are left, and these are dispersed in twenty-six separate locations; even the largest herd, a group of twenty in a national park, is probably not a self-sustaining population.

This animal was captured in the wild in 1987 and is part of a captive population totaling sixteen animals worldwide. Half of that group is in a single zoo where the animals, locked in cages and corrals, spend their days trilling back and forth to each other with voices like those of whales.

We drive up the Malay Peninsula. I am unprepared for this landscape: instead of tropical forest, the place is an endless succession of oil palm and rubber tree plantations. The few vestiges of original vegetation which fringe distant ridges are being loaded onto the trucks that roar past us down the highway.

Faced with a scene like this, it would be easy to blame corporate greed and the ignorance of local peasantry. Yet neither corporations nor local peasants are ultimately responsible for the consumer demand that is replacing rhino habitat with industrial trees. We—individually, one by one—are. Without an understanding of that fact, no real progress is possible on the problem of endangered species and the larger problem of our endangered environment.

SUMATRAN RHINOCEROS

"Mas Merah."
Photographed October 23, 1989, at the Malacca Zoo, Malacca, Malaysia. Adult female, age unknown.
USFWS Endangered,
IUCN Endangered,
CITES I

Like most animals, rhinos need to learn the sex act. But since Clyde was wild-caught as an infant and spent his life in either Switzerland's Basel Zoo or the Columbus Zoo, he never saw an experienced male in action, nor, until recently, did he ever get to mate with a practiced female. He was thus too rough, and his attempts at reproduction failed.

But in this world of rapidly fading rhinoceros life, his sperm is a precious resource. Not long after this photograph was made, a sexually experienced female became available for Clyde, and zoo-keepers have high hopes for a successful union.

BLACK RHINOCEROS

"Clyde." Photographed May 23, 1989, at the Columbus Zoo, Powell, Ohio. Thirty-seven-year-old male.
USFWS Endangered,
IUCN Endangered,
CITES I

"Jordy." Photographed
February 11, 1989, at the
Lowry Park Zoo, Tampa,
Florida. Six-year-old male.
USFWS Endangered,
IUCN Endangered,
CITES I

GREAT INDIAN RHINOCEROS

Nearly half of the thirty-six Indian rhinos in North American zoos, including Jordy, are descended from a single ancestor. To avoid inbreeding with his own bloodline, Jordy has been exiled from the other Indian rhinos with whom he previously lived, but there is some chance that he will someday return from this exile-within-exile and be paired with a mate fresh from the wild.

The day before we worked with Jordy, a female baboon in heat had sat on the background fabric, and he found her scent irresistible. He avidly sniffed and licked the background, all the while curling back his upper lip to expose a certain olfactory gland which plays a key part in breeding rituals. Our needs could not distract this rhino from his own, so we ended that session.

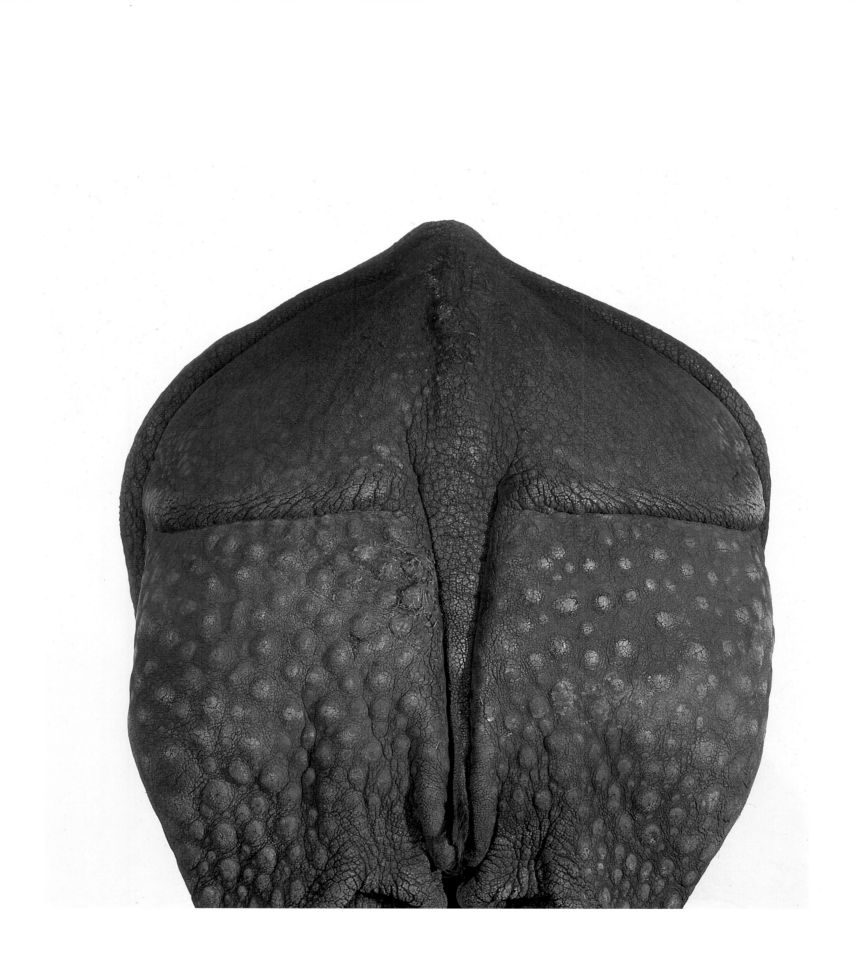

WHITE RHINOCEROS

"Ma." Photographed March
7, 1988, at Marine World
Africa, Vallejo, California.
Twenty-one-year-old
female.
USFWS Endangered,
IUCN Endangered,
CITES I

BLACK RHINOCEROS

"Macho." Photographed October 10, 1988, on a private ranch in south Texas. Twelve-year-old male.
USFWS Endangered,
IUCN Endangered,
CITES I

Said the ranch owner: "Don't mention the exact location of this animal. Nobody in Texas could do anything with a dead rhino, but a lot of people would love to say they killed one."

Of all the African animals, the black rhinoceros is one of those most threatened with extinction. In 1970, there were 60,000 black rhinos. Today, about 3,500 survive, and aggressive bands of poachers armed with automatic weapons are killing the last remaining herds at a rate that will make them extinct within a decade.

The primary cause for their decline is poaching. Macho's horns would retail for $40,000 to $50,000 on the black market. They would be sold to make Oriental folk medicines (aphrodisiacs, "heart tonics," stimulants), and dagger handles for the men of North Yemen. Local governments, beset by internal political and military crises, and sometimes ruled by officials surreptitiously profiting from the poaching, are unable or unwilling to intervene.

Macho's personality is more akin to that of a pet than to the stereotypical image of "awesome rhino." With a tender pink upper lip, he gently plucked Macintosh apples from my hand. Coltlike, he pranced around the corral on stiff legs. His only vocalization was a small squeak, much like that of a puppy.

As with so many other forms of hoofed African wildlife, the initial cause of the decline of this zebra was the European settlement of Africa. Ranchers were unable or unwilling to let wildlife compete for forage with their livestock, so "white hunters" killed hundreds of thousands of wild animals.

The Grevy's continues in decline throughout its arid, brushy habitat. The primary threat is the wildlife curio trade, which prizes the particular stripe pattern of this zebra above all others. The southward migration of the Sahara has dried up some of the habitat. And in that pathological way which men with guns sometimes have, the soldiers in Ethiopia's civil war indiscriminately and casually slaughter this animal just for the sake of emptying their guns.

Making a zebra photograph was troublesome because zebras, like elephants and tigers, are universal visual clichés. It seemed nearly impossible to make an image transcending normal perception enough to be interesting. But unforeseen circumstances intervened and led me to a solution.

A few days before our session with the Grevy's, I was badly bitten by fire ants and had a reaction acute enough to make me brood about my mortality. This was followed the next day by the news that a close friend who was seemingly healthy and strong was, in fact, terminally ill with cancer. I was struck by the notion that life, which we normally perceive as a solid surface surrounding us, was actually a kind of projection screen capable of

ripping open at any minute and letting us float through into whatever reality waits on the other side.

When we set up the shot in the zebra's corral, I simply made the picture that felt right at the time. It was not until later that I realized how the mortality issue had influenced visual intuition. The image of the moving zebra torso portrays an entity in motion to the other side of life's projection screen. The shadow lingering on the screen is a last glimpse of that entity before it flickers away and disappears entirely from view.

G R E V Y ' S   Z E B R A

Photographed October 17, 1988, at La Coma Ranch Red Gate, Edinburg, Texas. Adult male. USFWS Threatened, IUCN Endangered, CITES I

ASIAN CROCODILE

Photographed February
15, 1989, at Gatorland,
Orlando, Florida. Male,
age unknown.
CITES II

MORELET'S
CROCODILE

Photographed February
15, 1989, at Gatorland,
Orlando, Florida. Female,
age unknown.
USFWS Endangered,
IUCN Endangered,
CITES I

HUMBOLDT
PENGUIN

"Pepper." Photographed
May 16, 1989, at the
Cleveland Zoo, Cleveland,
Ohio. Five-year-old female.
IUCN Unknown, CITES I

G A L A P A G O S G I A N T T O R T O I S E

Photographed January 12, 1988, at Busch Gardens, Tampa, Florida. Age unknown, but measured in centuries.
USFWS Endangered, IUCN Vulnerable, CITES I

Giant tortoises are the most long-lived vertebrates on the planet. Though no one is certain how old they can become, their normal life span apparently reaches at least 150 to 175 years.

Nineteenth-century whalers and museum collectors wiped out huge numbers of the animals. The whalers were in pursuit of fresh meat to stave off scurvy, while the Victorian collectors, persuaded that collecting tortoises was fashionable, eradicated entire subspecies of the population. Domestic livestock forced the tortoise into marginal terrain and reduced its rate of reproductive success by stepping on or eating the reptile's eggs. Should the habitat be degraded in the future, extinction is almost certain, because tortoises reproduce poorly or not at all in captivity.

Though I could never prove it, I am certain these tortoises were having a conversation about us. Some sort of auditory phantom drifted through that room, a vibration usually too faint for me to be sure I actually heard it, but it would sometimes manifest itself as a quiet clicking sound. Couple that with the intelligence in those eyes and I could not avoid the sense that I was being judged.

ASIAN SMALL-CLAWED OTTER

The numbers and ecological vitality of the species are unknown, but scientists are fairly certain it is threatened and are attempting to collect more definitive data. Environmental pollution and habitat destruction appear to be the main threats to the animal.

This otter was in the frenzy of perpetual motion which typifies otters' lives: in the water, out of the water, back into the water and then under it, around and around and around in dizzying circles.

Photographed November 11, 1988, at Sea World of Texas, San Antonio, Texas. Adult male. IUCN Insufficiently known, CITES II

WEST INDIAN MANATEE

"Marina." Photographed
January 13, 1989, at Sea
World, Orlando, Florida.
Seven-year-old female.
USFWS Endangered,
IUCN Vulnerable

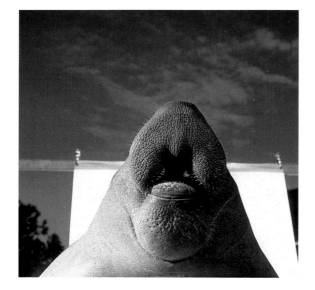

This mammal, which lives in warm coastal waters of the Caribbean and Atlantic from Florida to Brazil, sharply declined owing to hunting for its meat, hide, oil, and bones. During the Spanish conquest of Central and South America, large-scale slaughter provided meat for extended sea voyages; later, manatees were used to feed African slaves on Ca-ribbean sugar plantations. Commercial hunting is no longer a threat, but Latin American subsistence hunting still takes a significant toll.

Manatees are slow-moving animals much given to lolling just at the water's surface and munching on aquatic plants. In such a position they are barely visible and boats and barges regularly run into them or the propellers rip open the manatees' hides. This manatee was six months old when it was found orphaned at a Florida marina, its mother probably the victim of yet another collision.

Repeatedly, these animal images come from the dreamworld. They somehow inch across the threshold between the unconscious and the conscious and suddenly find ways of leaping onto silver grains of film. Marina is the incarnation of a dream animal which has visited me for years: a great dark anima-beast which I haul from the sea. At first, she is frightening and ugly, but in time becomes friendly and beautiful.

And that is this manatee of reality. She is gentle and quiet, happy to loll at pool's edge and feel me scratch her skin, talk to her, and shake her blubber. Her snout is soft leather, like deerskin, but the rest of her body has the rough tautness of a football made from sandpaper. She sleeps, then blinks an eye open and slips back beneath the waves as unexpectedly as she came.

FLORIDA PANTHER

Photographed January 27,
1989. Owned by Wildlife
Rescue, Tampa, Florida.
Three-year-old male.
USFWS Endangered,
IUCN Endangered,
CITES I

Though there is considerable uncertainty about the wild population of Florida panthers, biologists believe that probably only thirty to fifty of these cats survive in the wild today. Overhunting, trapping, and poisoning caused the panthers' decline in earlier decades, but habitat destruction is now their main problem: prime Everglades habitat is continually being whittled away by condominiums, recreation camps, and water diversion projects. Illegal hunting and roadkill are other problems for the cats—just the day before our session, another wild panther was killed by a car on a south Florida highway.

We made this image in a rented studio on a dreary side street in Tampa. In spite of our initial worries about being locked up in a small room with a large and sharp-toothed cat, the biggest problem we encountered with this elegant animal was that, like ordinary house cats, all he really wanted to do was sleep. Even offers of horsemeat rarely held his interest.

Just before this exposure was made, he drifted off into yet another nap. But a noise offstage caught his attention, and he gave me a piercing, haunting look.

125

OCELOT

"Fiera." Photographed
May 24, 1989, at the
Cincinnati Zoo, Cincinnati,
Ohio. Fourteen-month-old
female.
USFWS Endangered,
IUCN Vulnerable,
CITES II

Ocelots are the most hunted cats in Latin America because, as one might guess, the fashion industry prizes their fur. They have recently lost an enormous amount of tropical forest habitat to human settlement and agricultural activity, though they do still thrive in undeveloped areas. People who like exotic pets are another threat: capturing kittens so they can be transformed into acceptable pets requires killing their mothers.

Fiera was born in captivity of parents many generations removed from wild life.

"Sarah." Photographed
May 22, 1989, at the
Columbus Zoo, Powell,
Ohio. Six-month-old
female.

SERVAL CAT

Sarah is virtually identical to the nearly
extinct Barbary serval cat.

CHEETAH

Our technological civilization has an unfortunate habit of reducing the world to quantifiable bits and bytes while missing the meaning of the whole. This image refers to that syndrome. Its unofficial title is "Binary Reduction."

"Hashim." Photographed
May 22 and 23, 1989, at the
Columbus Zoo, Powell,
Ohio. Thirty-month-old
male.
USFWS Endangered,
IUCN Vulnerable,
CITES I

GRIZZLY BEAR

Though grizzlies once roamed much of North America west of the Mississippi, the only thriving populations are now in Alaska and Canada. For the most part, grizzlies in the Lower 48 states are barely managing to survive in a few islands of favorable habitat, including the ecosystem in and around Yellowstone National Park.

The last known grizzly south of Yellowstone died in 1979 in a remote section of the Colorado Rockies. The bear, suffering a wound inflicted by bow hunters, attacked a hunting guide who chased her into a thicket. The guide stabbed her to death with an arrow. A species called the Mexican grizzly bear exists only as a phantom: it is still on the endangered lists, but no one has definitely seen a Mexican grizzly alive in the wild during the past quarter century. Though biologists hope for its survival, it is almost certainly extinct.

It is stunning to have Bailey walk into the small room. His claws click on the white linoleum of the set as he tours around in that way animals have—sniffing, looking, touching with his nose. Then he comes to me.

I crouch on my haunches, at eye level with him. He gets bigger. And bigger. And bigger. When it seems that his head fills my entire field of view, I feel his hot breath. It is not breath exactly, because that gives too gentle an impression, but something more akin to wind—panting, rushing in warm waves around my face. Against everything I know to be true about this bear, and against all the mental coaching I have given myself, he sends a shudder to the core of my psyche.

Here is Bear: power incarnate. The beauty of this power is that it exists entirely within him—not as a result of tools or inventions or surrogates, but because it is his essence. Though he can wreak total destruction anytime he likes, he chooses to act with delicacy. Yet even now, I feel that breath.

The vast majority of chimpanzees live in Zaire and Gabon, with scattered populations in the tropical forests of equatorial Africa. Chimpanzee populations have been decimated by meat hunters, habitat loss, and the illegal capture of live animals for medical and pharmaceutical research. (To catch just a single juvenile from a chimp family, poachers kill all the adults.) The genes of chimps are 99 percent identical to human genes, making them more similar to us than to gorillas.

Beau was born in Busch Gardens, as was his mother. His father was brought from the African jungles in June, 1964. In my mind I see an image of refugees trudging through the mud, fleeing the ravages of warfare. For the animals it is the same, their families blown apart by the great war sweeping through their homeland, leaving the tattered remnants to drift on the winds of fate into foreign lands.

With Beau, more than with nearly any other animal I have photographed, I get an intense impression of his Beingness, of his presence. It would normally be said that he is "so quick to learn," implying that he is remarkably like a human, but not as good. In fact, he learns the hand positions I ask of him as rapidly as would any human asked to do unfamiliar motions—and, allowing for the enormous language barrier, I would say he actually learns faster than would a human. Gently, he always wants to reach out and touch me.

"Beau." Photographed January 23, 1989, at Busch Gardens, Tampa, Florida. Nine-year-old male. USFWS Endangered, IUCN Vulnerable, CITES I

CHIMPANZEE

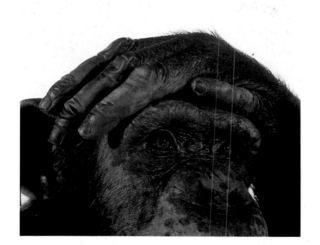

Koko is the world-famous gorilla who speaks American Sign Language. The first words keeper Penny Patterson translated for me were:

"Penny, do you have any candy?" (No)

"Does he have any candy?" (No)

Koko is at first reluctant to enter the room where we have set up the background and lights. But she is clearly curious about the newcomer in her space, so I crouch down near the backdrop to draw her in. That does it. She walks over on her knuckles and doesn't stop until her chestnut-brown eyes are four inches away from mine.

She stares, nostrils flaring, her breath fanning my face, her bulk and presence blotting out all other space. I am unprepared for such immediate, frank curiosity and am scared. Raising her black finger, she gently taps my temple, then my cheek, then plucks at the small mole below my eye. She lifts my right arm and licks it. Then, putting one arm around my shoulder and the other on the back of my neck, she pulls my face to her chest.

The contact across the species barrier left me spinning. I have not yet absorbed it all.

LOWLAND GORILLA

"Koko." Photographed July 1, 1989, at the Gorilla Foundation, Woodside, California. Seventeen-year-old female.
USFWS Endangered, IUCN Vulnerable, CITES I

GOLDEN LION TAMARIN

"Nugget." Photographed January 23, 1989, at Busch Gardens, Tampa, Florida. Eight-year-old male. USFWS Endangered, IUCN Endangered, CITES I

The phenomenal human population explosion in China's Szechuan province (45 million to 150 million since 1900) has fragmented pandas into approximately twelve separate groups totaling 1,000 animals. Because even the largest of these population fragments is much too small to be reproductively viable, and because pandas' breeding success in captivity is almost nil, the species may be well on its way to extinction.

Poachers continually whittle away the remaining animals in order to supply the black market: the greatest demand is from the Japanese, who pay up to $20,000 for a panda pelt.

GIANT PANDA

"Wei-Wei." Photographed October 31, 1989, at the Shanghai Acrobatic Theater, Shanghai, China. Sixteen-year-old male. USFWS Endangered, IUCN Rare, CITES I

The planning for this image of the only tractable panda in the world seemed to go on forever. By the time we actually reached Shanghai, "panda" had assumed larger-than-life dimensions in my mind. The real panda, however, was a surprisingly small animal curled in the corner of a tiny cage in the corner of a tiny room in a dreary back alley, an animal as beautiful and surreal as animals come, but a flesh-and-blood being nonetheless.

"Buck." Photographed
September 22, 1989, at
Steve Martin's Working
Wildlife, Lockwood
Valley, California.
Six-year-old male.
USFWS Endangered,
IUCN Vulnerable,
CITES I

GRAY WOLF

The brunt of Western hostility toward
animal nature was borne by canine and
ursine predators in general, but the wolf
family took the worst beating of all.
Wolves personified everything wrong
with nonhuman forces in the world, sym-
bolizing the "howling wilderness" that
every civilized person was duty-bound to
suppress.